YOUR
BODY ON
GLUTEN

BY MIKE DOWNS

CONTENT CONSULTANT
Debbie Fetter, PhD
Lecturer (PSOE), Department of Nutrition
University of California, Davis

Cover image: Bagels are a comm

Core Library

abdocorelibrary.com

Published by Abdo Publishing, a division of ABDO, PO Box 398166, Minneapolis, Minnesota 55439. Copyright © 2020 by Abdo Consulting Group, Inc. International copyrights reserved in all countries. No part of this book may be reproduced in any form without written permission from the publisher. Core Library™ is a trademark and logo of Abdo Publishing.

Printed in the United States of America, North Mankato, Minnesota
022019
092019

THIS BOOK CONTAINS
RECYCLED MATERIALS

Cover Photo: Brent Hofacker/Shutterstock Images
Interior Photos: Brent Hofacker/Shutterstock Images, 1; Shutterstock Images, 4–5, 12–13, 18, 20–21, 34–35, 43; iStockphoto, 7, 22–23 (background), 25, 26–27, 32, 45; Sheila Fitzgerald/ Shutterstock Images, 9, 37; Molekuul/Science Source, 17; Dr. Keith Wheeler/Science Source, 22–23 (foreground); Cordelia Molloy/Science Source, 28; Adam Calaitzis/iStockphoto, 39

Editor: Marie Pearson
Series Designer: Claire Vanden Branden

Library of Congress Control Number: 2018965966

Publisher's Cataloging-in-Publication Data

Names: Downs, Mike, author.
Title: Your body on gluten / by Mike Downs
Description: Minneapolis, Minnesota : Abdo Publishing, 2020 | Series: Nutrition and your body | Includes online resources and index.
Identifiers: ISBN 9781532118852 (lib. bdg.) | ISBN 9781532173035 (ebook) | ISBN 9781644940761 (pbk.)
Subjects: LCSH: Gluten--Use in cooking--Juvenile literature. | Food--Gluten content--Juvenile literature. | Gluten-free diet--Juvenile literature. | Food--Health aspects--Juvenile literature.
Classification: DDC 613.20--dc23

CONTENTS

GLUTEN AND YOU

José watches closely as the pizza dough flies up toward the ceiling. It spins in a floppy circle. The chef holds her hands out, waiting. She skillfully catches the dough as it returns. Then she hurls it back up into the air. With each throw, the dough stretches and widens.

Finally, the disc of dough is the right size. The chef throws it on the counter. The elastic, stretchy dough is ready for toppings. She layers the dough with sauce, cheese, and pepperoni. She slides it in the oven. José sniffs the wonderful aroma of cooking pizza. His mouth starts to salivate. When the pizza arrives at the

Pizza dough is often made of wheat flour, which has gluten.

table, he quickly grabs a piece. Folding the warm, soft crust in half, he takes a chewy bite.

As he devours the delicious meal, he's probably not thinking about gluten. But he's eating it. Gluten is a mixture of proteins. It's found in wheat and other grains. It gives the dough its flexible, stretchy quality. That gluten is now heading straight into José's body.

THROUGH THE DIGESTIVE SYSTEM

From the moment he starts to salivate, José's digestive system goes to work. He chews the pizza. It mixes with

Pizza is a popular food. It can be made with many toppings, but it usually has a flour crust.

his saliva. The pizza softens into a squishy lump. His tongue pushes the lump into his throat. From there it moves to his stomach. The stomach breaks down the food into its basic parts. Those parts become a liquid mixture.

The liquid leaves his stomach and enters his intestines. His intestines absorb the nutrients his body needs. The leftovers are removed as waste products in the form of urine and stool.

Most people's bodies don't have trouble with gluten. They can happily eat pizza without a problem. But that's not always the case. Some people have a bad reaction to gluten. The gluten irritates their small intestine. They can get abdominal pain or diarrhea. Gluten might even damage their digestive system. These people need to avoid gluten.

But most people don't want to avoid pizza. They search for gluten-free substitutes. The words *gluten free* pop up at restaurants and stores everywhere.

With a growing demand for gluten-free foods, many companies are now making gluten-free products.

GLUTEN EVERYWHERE

People who can't tolerate gluten eat gluten-free food. But it's not easy. Gluten is everywhere. It's in chewy pizza dough and freshly baked bread. It's in cereals, bagels, pasta, and crackers. Gluten is found in most bakeries, restaurants, coffee shops, and fast-food outlets. This is a huge problem for those with gluten troubles. That's why they're searching for substitutes.

WHAT DOES *GLUTEN FREE* MEAN?

In general, foods without wheat, rye, or barley are gluten free. But some foods contain a tiny bit of gluten. They aren't always considered gluten free. The US Food and Drug Administration set a standard in 2013. As long as a food contains less than 20 parts per million of gluten, the product can be labeled gluten free. Parts per million is a measurement. For example, someone might have 1 million grains of sand. Most grains may be tan. But there are 20 brown grains. The brown grains would make up 20 parts per million.

Some foods are naturally gluten free. Others need to use alternative ingredients. But most alternative ingredients do not have gluten's stretchable qualities.

To get a better grasp on the problems gluten can cause, it's worth taking a closer look at what gluten is. That will lead to more understanding of the steps that individuals, doctors, and food companies are taking to deal with the issue.

STRAIGHT TO THE
SOURCE

In a 2014 interview, nutritionist Alessio Fasano talked about people who go on gluten-free diets even if they don't have gluten sensitivity:

> *The immune system seems to see the gluten as a component of bacteria and deploys weapons to attack it, and creates some collateral damage we call inflammation.*
>
> *But our bodies are engaging in this war all the time, and for the vast majority of us, there's a controlled reaction, the enemies are defeated and nothing happens. . . .*
>
> *So if you argue on that basis that we should all go gluten free, it's like saying that we should all get rid of germs or bacteria. That's ridiculous. Our bodies deal with bacteria all the time.*

> Source: Elaine Watson. "Dr. Alessio Fasano Speaks Out about Celebrity Gluten-Bashing, Celiac Disease Research." *Celiac Disease Foundation*. Celiac Disease Foundation, February 3, 2014. Web. Accessed October 4, 2018.

Consider Your Audience

Read this passage carefully. Adapt his statement for a different audience, such as your friends. Write a blog post explaining his point of view. How does your post differ from the original text and why?

WHAT IS GLUTEN?

Gluten is a cluster of proteins. It's found in the seeds of wheat, barley, and rye. It's also found in lesser-known seeds such as spelt and einkorn. Gluten is used as food for the germ inside the seed. The germ is the part that grows into a new plant. Gluten normally gets into food because the seeds are ground into flour. Wheat seeds, also called wheat berries, are most commonly used for this purpose. Flour used to make dough still contains the gluten.

Wheat is one of the most commonly used grains with gluten.

GLUTEN IN WHEAT

Wheat is the most popular grain used for flour. The wheat seed is made up of three main parts. The outer layer is the bran. The inner food-storage part is the endosperm. And the part that sprouts is the germ. Gluten is in the endosperm. When wheat seeds are ground into flour, the gluten remains in the flour.

Gluten makes up approximately 12 percent of all-purpose flour. It's an important 12 percent. The gluten makes flour sticky when water is added. It strengthens the dough. It makes dough elastic. Gluten also helps the dough rise when it's baked.

Gluten works like a gluey component of dough. In fact, the English word *glue* came from the Latin word *gluten*.

THE GLUTEN PROTEIN

Seeds use gluten protein as food. Human bodies also use proteins as food. Proteins are very important to health. They're used to build hair and fingernails. Skin, bones, and muscles also use proteins. Proteins help transport oxygen in the blood. They help fight infection.

Proteins make up approximately 16 percent of a man's body weight. That percentage is slightly less in women.

Proteins do many wonderful things. It can be difficult to understand why gluten would cause a problem. The answer begins with gluten's makeup.

The gluten in wheat is made of two parts: glutenin and gliadin. Glutenin is easily digested. The body breaks it down into parts called amino acids. These are the building blocks of proteins. Then the body uses the amino acids as needed.

Gliadin is not easily digested. The digestive system can't break it down into smaller amino acids. For some people, the undigested gliadin causes a

MAKING PROTEINS

All proteins are made up of amino acids. Proteins are a vital part of the human body. People need amino acids to build proteins. The body can make some amino acids itself. These are called nonessential amino acids. Other amino acids can only come from certain foods. These are called essential amino acids.

problem. It creates inflammation in the small intestine. In these people, the undigested gliadin is treated as a threat. The body's immune system attacks it. This can cause serious health issues.

THE TROUBLE WITH GLIADIN

Gliadin can cause problems during digestion. So it is important to understand a bit more about the digestive system and how it works. The digestive system is made of several organs. These organs take food and convert it into nutrients the body needs. The stomach uses muscle action and chemicals to break the food down into small molecules. The stomach then sends this into the small intestine.

The small intestine continues the digestion process. It's also where most of the nutrients are absorbed. The inside lining of the small intestine is covered with millions of very small projections. These projections are called villi. They have tiny blood vessels in them that

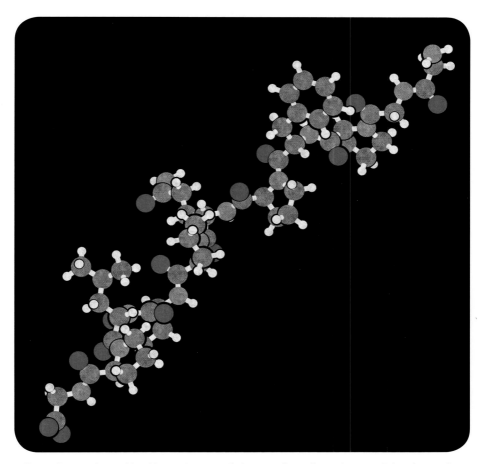

Like glutenin, gliadin, *pictured*, is made of amino acids, but the body can't break it down like it can glutenin.

absorb the nutrients. If the villi are damaged, the body has trouble absorbing the nutrients it needs.

Gliadin is a group of molecules held tightly together. A person's body can't break gliadin down into smaller amino acids. It cannot be fully digested.

DAMAGED VILLI

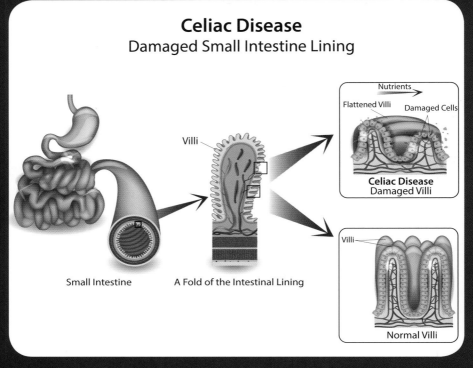

Celiac Disease
Damaged Small Intestine Lining

Nutrients

Flattened Villi   Damaged Cells

Celiac Disease
Damaged Villi

Villi

Small Intestine

A Fold of the Intestinal Lining

Villi

Normal Villi

The villi in the small intestine help absorb nutrients. How do they look different in a person with celiac disease? Why do you think the damaged villi absorb fewer nutrients? Does the graphic help you better understand what is happening?

That sounds bad. But it isn't normally a problem. Most people eat lots of foods their bodies can't break down. These foods are disposed of as waste. Most people's bodies simply treat gliadin as waste. They eat gluten-filled foods without any bad effects.

But some people have a different experience. They have a bad reaction to the gliadin. When gliadin travels through the digestive system, it irritates the small intestine. It causes uncomfortable symptoms. Some people's bodies treat gliadin as a foreign invader. Their bodies send antibodies to attack the gliadin. This causes inflammation of the small intestine. It damages the villi. This serious problem is called celiac disease.

EXPLORE ONLINE

Chapter Two explains that gluten is a protein. The website below explains proteins in more detail. Does this help increase your understanding? If so, what information helped you better understand?

KIDSHEALTH: LEARNING ABOUT PROTEINS
abdocorelibrary.com/gluten

REACTIONS TO GLUTEN

There are two primary diseases linked to gluten. The most serious is celiac disease. It affects approximately one in every 100 people in the United States. That is 1 percent of the population. The other is non-celiac gluten sensitivity (NCGS). This affects approximately 6 percent of the population. Both problems cause symptoms such as bloating, stomach pain, diarrhea, fatigue, and bad-smelling stool. The two diseases are difficult to tell apart. Most people who have celiac disease don't even know it. And many people who have these symptoms blame it on some other cause.

People whose bodies react to gluten may show symptoms for a long time before doctors figure out that gluten is the cause.

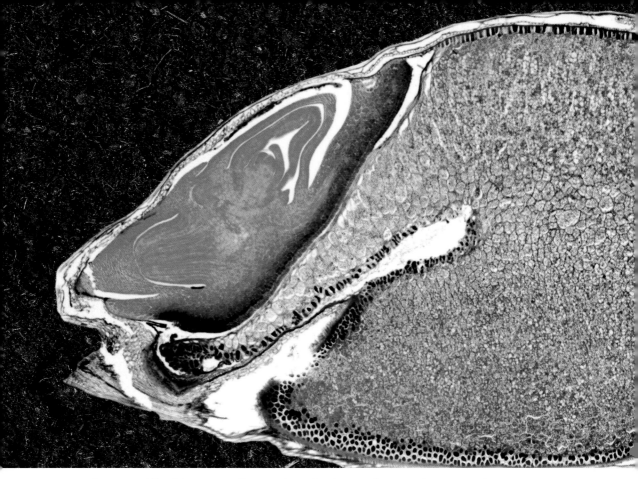

A magnified image of a grain of wheat shows the part the new plant grows out of, *left, deep red*, and the part that contains food for the plant, including gluten, *right, blue and red*.

A separate problem is wheat or gluten allergies. These are completely different from celiac disease and gluten sensitivity.

CELIAC DISEASE

Celiac disease is the most damaging problem caused by gluten. It is an autoimmune disorder. This means

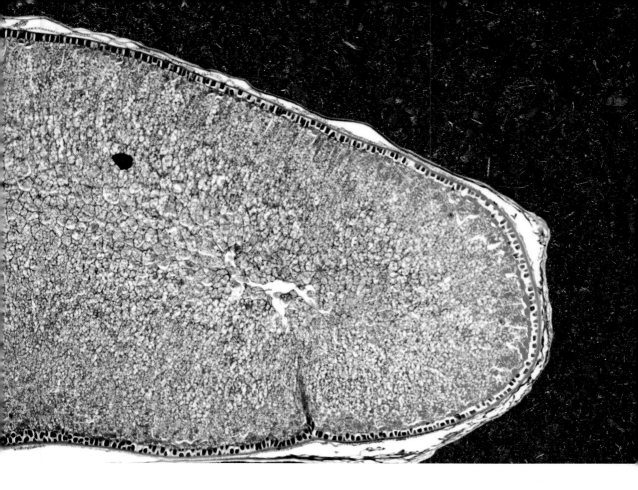

the body attacks and damages its own tissue. When someone with celiac disease eats gluten, the body's immune system attacks it. The immune system treats gluten as an invader. This attack damages the villi in the small intestine. Damaged villi have difficulty absorbing the nutrition the body needs. These attacks also cause inflammation and swelling. This can further

WHY VILLI?

Millions of villi stick up inside the small intestine. They're there for a good reason. If the inside of the intestine were smooth, there wouldn't be much space to absorb nutrients. The projecting villi increase the surface area inside the small intestine. The villi even have their own projections. These little hairs are called microvilli. With all the villi and microvilli sticking up, there are plenty of places to absorb nutrients into the body.

affect the entire body. Celiac disease can lead to serious long-term problems.

The symptoms of celiac disease can be different for children and adults. A young person might have diarrhea, gas, bloating, and other stomach problems. Adults can have some of the same symptoms. They may also have skin rashes, heartburn, and joint pain. These are only a few in a long list of possible symptoms. Celiac disease increases the risk of other problems. People with celiac disease have a higher chance of developing other autoimmune diseases. An early diagnosis helps

People with celiac need to be careful their gluten-free food does not get gluten on it. It is safest to use different surfaces and utensils than those used to make food with gluten.

prevent this from happening. But that diagnosis isn't easy to make.

The first step in diagnosing celiac disease is to get a blood test. The blood test will look for a

Oats do not naturally have gluten, but they often come in contact with wheat during production. People with celiac need to look for oat products labeled *gluten free*.

specific antibody. People without the antibody do not have celiac disease. However, it's possible to have the antibody but not the disease. If the blood test is positive, another test is needed. A doctor will take a sample of the small intestine. This sample will show if

there has been any damage to the villi. If the villi are damaged, then celiac disease is present.

The causes of celiac disease aren't yet fully known. But there are a few indicators. Celiac disease typically affects people who have certain genes. Genes include

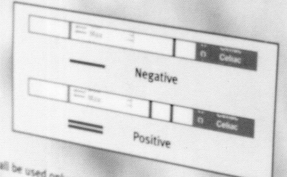

Biocard ™ Celiac Test

A rapid and sensitive home test for the detection of celiac disease associated IgA autoantibodies from a fingertip blood sample.

Negative

Positive

Cat.no. 3-028-401

Pat. PCT/FI 02/00340

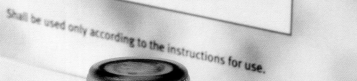

Shall be used only according to the instructions for use.

ANIBio

the DNA that people get from their parents. Genes influence a person's traits such as hair color or height. About one-third of the population has the genes that make it possible for them to have celiac disease. These genes may be passed down within families. A person with a close family member who has celiac disease is about 10 percent more likely to have the disease.

To have a reaction to gluten, a person first needs to eat gluten. Then his or her body must have an autoimmune reaction to it. Sometimes people eat gluten for years before getting the disease. The disease might be triggered by mental stress. Events such as surgery or viral infections could also trigger it.

GLUTEN SENSITIVITY

Celiac disease is the most damaging disease related to gluten. But it's not the only one. Millions of people have bad reactions to gluten. But they don't cause the serious long-term damage that celiac disease can cause.

Some people order at-home kits to test their blood for the antibody that can indicate celiac.

These people have NCGS. In these cases, the symptoms may show up soon after eating gluten. The symptoms may be the same as those for celiac disease. The important difference is that NCGS does not damage villi. A person might get abdominal pain or other symptoms. But the small intestine is not harmed.

Another term that people use is *self-reported gluten sensitivity*. This refers to the fact that many people decide on their own that they're sensitive to gluten. It may or may not be true. It could be another

LONG-TERM DANGER

The longer a person lives with undiagnosed celiac disease, the higher the chances of long-term damage to the body. But most people who have celiac disease don't even know it. The average person waits six to ten years for an accurate diagnosis. Combine this with the fact that celiac disease is one of the most common lifelong diseases in the world. That means millions of people worldwide are at risk.

problem. But some of them start a gluten-free diet hoping to improve their symptoms.

Determining the cause of different symptoms is like piecing together a puzzle. Frequently, guessing is involved. Doctors put the pieces together. Then doctors and patients can figure out the best course of action.

WHEAT ALLERGIES

Allergies can also cause people to avoid foods with gluten. People can have an allergic reaction to something in the wheat. Allergic reactions are completely different from celiac disease or gluten sensitivity. Someone with celiac disease might not feel symptoms. But every time that person eats gluten, it damages the small intestine. Gluten sensitivity may be uncomfortable. But it's not dangerous.

An allergic reaction is different. It can happen immediately after or within a few hours of eating wheat. The symptoms might include itching, rash, headaches, congestion, or diarrhea. It can also cause a very

THE DIAGNOSIS DILEMMA

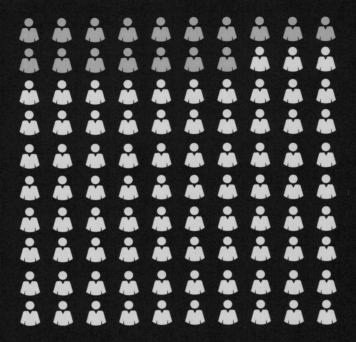

■ Diagnosed with Celiac   ■ Misdiagnosed or Undiagnosed

One of the biggest problems with celiac disease is figuring out who has it. It has symptoms similar to those of many other health issues. Doctors may misdiagnose the problem if someone has a stomachache or diarrhea. For every 100 people who have celiac disease, how many know about it?

dangerous reaction called anaphylaxis. Symptoms of anaphylaxis are trouble breathing or swallowing, chest pain, dizziness, or fainting.

STRAIGHT TO THE
SOURCE

Dr. Stephen Wangen talks about early detection of celiac disease and NCGS:

> *It is still important to emphasize that the sooner gluten intolerance is discovered, the better. Infants or children whose intolerance is found early will be much healthier and are likely to continue to be healthier throughout life. They will absorb nutrients better and will be much closer to optimal health than they would have been otherwise. Studies have also shown that once gluten is removed from the diet, children who have suffered from poor growth tend to catch up. And the younger the child is at diagnosis, the better the chance that he or she will catch up. Long term health starts in our infancy and continues throughout our lives. There should be no doubt that the earlier a gluten intolerance is discovered, the better off a person will be.*

Source: Stephen Wangen. *Healthier without Wheat*. Seattle: Innate Health, 2009. Chapter 8. *Google Books*. Web. Accessed October 4, 2018.

Back It Up

The author is trying to make a specific point. Write a paragraph describing what his point is. List two pieces of evidence he uses to support his view.

WHAT TO DO ABOUT GLUTEN

Seven percent of people report having gluten sensitivity. That means 93 percent don't have a problem with gluten at all. For that 93 percent, a normal, healthy diet is the best option. Advertising by food companies might suggest that a gluten-free diet is healthier. But there's no scientific evidence to support this. In fact, starting a gluten-free diet without reason could be a bad idea.

Just because a food is gluten free does not mean it's healthy. For people without gluten sensitivity, eating gluten free can actually be less healthy than not avoiding gluten. It is also

Rice is a common substitute for grains containing gluten.

more expensive. A gluten-free diet means avoiding wheat and its fiber. This fiber helps the digestive process. This fiber would need to be replaced with other grains or fibers. Processed gluten-free foods can also have fewer nutrients. They don't always have added vitamins like breads and cereals made with wheat do. Processed gluten-free foods also tend to be higher in fats and sugars. However, naturally gluten-free foods such as lean meats, vegetables, and fruits are a part of any healthy diet.

So there is no reason for people without gluten sensitivity to go gluten free. But millions of people do need to avoid gluten. For them, there is both bad and good news.

BAD NEWS, GOOD NEWS

First, the bad news: gluten is everywhere. These are a few of the foods that gluten-sensitive eaters have to avoid: pasta, pizza, bread, cookies, cakes, flour tortillas,

Packaged gluten-free foods can have just as much or more sugar than their gluten counterparts.

Betty Crocker™

yellow Gluten Free cake mix

no artificial colors
or preservatives

ENLARGED TO
SHOW DETAIL
SERVING
SUGGESTION

PER 1/9 PACKAGE

180 CALORIES	0g SAT FAT	135mg SODIUM	20g TOTAL SUGARS
	0% DV	0% DV	

SEE NUTRITION FACTS

NET WT 15 OZ (425g)

PER 1

110 CALORIES

37

HIDDEN GLUTEN

Naturally gluten-free foods may still contain gluten. Manufacturers may add gluten to products that are canned, frozen, or processed. Sauces, gravies, processed meats, potato chips, and soups can also have gluten. If a label shows wheat, barley, rye, triticale, malt, or yeast, it definitely has gluten. But this is not a complete list.

cereal, bagels, crackers, pancakes. The list goes on. These are easy to guess because they contain flour. But other products are trickier.

Gluten can also be found in soy sauce, salad dressing, veggie burgers, potato chips, and gravy.

Foods without gluten can be contaminated if they're processed in the same place as foods with gluten. And gluten is not only in food products. Gluten can be in lip balm, vitamins, and other supplements.

Now for the good news. There are plenty of naturally gluten-free foods. These include fresh fruits and vegetables, beans, seafood, meats, and most dairy products. Also, food companies want to make money.

The number of gluten-free products continues to rise.

They're always looking for new and growing markets. Gluten-free food is just that.

The growing market is good for gluten-sensitive people. New gluten-free products appear in supermarkets every day. Gluten-sensitive eaters can now enjoy all the gluten-filled foods listed previously.

GLOBALLY GLUTEN FREE

In 2016, the global gluten-free market was valued at nearly $15 billion. It is forecasted to grow more than 9 percent a year. With many people buying gluten-free food, companies are rushing to introduce new products. Manufacturers are trying to make foods that taste better to help them compete. This is great news for anyone who eats gluten-free food.

They just need to track down the gluten-free versions.

THE GLUTEN SOLUTION

Gluten might not affect your personal health. But it affects others. Some people have to think about gluten at school lunchrooms, restaurants, and the grocery store. Friends may have gluten-free diets. Knowing about gluten gives you the ability to understand others whose bodies cannot handle gluten. You can be more aware of what they can eat and what they have to avoid.

Knowing about gluten can help you too. You can understand that most people do not have an issue with gluten. They can enjoy all the benefits of gluten. But for those whose bodies react badly to gluten, there are other options. Some taste just as good as foods with gluten!

FURTHER EVIDENCE

Chapter Four explains that there are lots of foods and other products with gluten. What was one of the main points of this chapter? What evidence is included to support this point? Read the article at the website below. Does the information on the website support the main point of the chapter? Does it present new evidence?

CELIAC DISEASE FOUNDATION: SOURCES OF GLUTEN
abdocorelibrary.com/gluten

FAST FACTS

- Gluten is found in most products that contain chewy dough. Gluten makes the dough elastic and strong.

- Wheat is the grain most commonly used in flour and in food products. Gluten is in wheat, barley, and rye.

- Gluten is a cluster of proteins with two parts: glutenin and gliadin. The digestive system cannot completely break down gliadin.

- Some people have a disease in which their immune system attacks gliadin and damages the small intestine. This is called celiac disease.

- About 7 percent of the population has some type of sensitivity to gluten.

- Health problems caused by gluten and wheat are hard to diagnose because they have symptoms similar to other medical problems.

- Gluten is found in many food products. Any product containing wheat, barley, or rye will have gluten. Gluten is sometimes added to processed foods that did not originally contain gluten.

- Some products that are naturally gluten free include fruits, vegetables, meat, fish, beans, and nuts.

- The gluten-free market is booming. More gluten-free food products are being developed every day.

STOP AND
THINK

Tell the Tale
Chapter Four explains that gluten is everywhere. Write 200 words about the foods you eat that might have gluten. Then explain what substitute foods you might eat if you had to avoid gluten. Would you miss having the original foods?

Surprise Me
Chapter One talked about how gluten makes dough chewy. After reading this book, what two or three facts about gluten's presence in food did you find most surprising? Write a few sentences about each fact. Why did you find each fact surprising?

Dig Deeper
After reading this book, what questions do you still have about gluten? With an adult's help, find a few reliable sources that can help you answer your questions. Write a paragraph about what you learned.

Say What?

Learning about gluten and some of its effects can mean learning a lot of new vocabulary. Find five words in this book that you've never heard before. Use a dictionary to find out what they mean. Then write the meanings in your own words, and use each word in a new sentence.

GLOSSARY

anaphylaxis
an allergic reaction, with symptoms including trouble breathing, trouble swallowing, chest pain, or dizziness

antibody
a special protein in the body that fights off foreign substances

diagnosis
the confirmation from a doctor of a specific cause of certain symptoms

digestive system
a group of organs that work together to turn food into fuel for the body

immune system
a system that protects the body from disease

inflammation
a swelling or redness caused by a bad, or adverse, reaction

molecule
the smallest unit of a chemical compound

nutrient
something in food that helps people, animals, and plants live and grow

processed
having gone through manufacturing

salivate
to make saliva in your mouth

symptom
a reaction the body has to a problem, such as vomiting, diarrhea, or a stomachache

ONLINE RESOURCES

To learn more about your body on gluten, visit our free resource websites below.

Core Library
CONNECTION
FREE! COMMON CORE MULTIMEDIA RESOURCES

Visit **abdocorelibrary.com** or scan this QR code for free Common Core resources for teachers and students, including vetted activities, multimedia, and booklinks, for deeper subject comprehension.

Booklinks
NONFICTION NETWORK
FREE! ONLINE NONFICTION RESOURCES

Visit **abdobooklinks.com** or scan this QR code for free additional online weblinks for further learning. These links are routinely monitored and updated to provide the most current information available.

LEARN MORE

Lusted, Marcia Amidon. *Gluten-Free and Other Special Diets*. Minneapolis, MN: Abdo Publishing, 2016. Print.

INDEX

About the Author

Mike Downs is an author, a pilot, and the father of three great kids. He loves to write and go on adventures. He also loves pizza, with or without the gluten.